# What the Bible Says about God, You and How You Can Know Him

*A.W. Tozer*

*CHRISTIAN PUBLICATIONS, INC.*
*CAMP HILL, PENNSYLVANIA*

CHRISTIAN PUBLICATIONS, Inc.
3825 Hartzdale Drive
Camp Hill, Pennsylvania 17011
www.cpi-horizon.com

ISBN: 0-87509-786-3



98 99 00 01 02 5 4 3 2 1

Printed in the United States of America

Unless otherwise indicated, Scripture taken from the King James Version of the Bible

"What the Bible Says" originally appeared in the *Alliance Witness* [now *Alliance Life*], September 5, 1962 issue.

"The Bible: The Book of Life" is taken from *We Travel an Appointed Way* by A.W. Tozer, compiled by Harry Verploegh, © 1988 by Christian Publications, Inc.

# What the Bible Says

The Bible is a big book; or more accurately it is a library composed of sixty-six books. Some of them are short and some long, but taken together they make a book of about 1,000 to 1,400 pages, depending upon the size of the print.

Of course not many people want to read a book that large, so the Bible doesn't get read as much as it once did. And is that good or bad? Is the Bible an old classic, good enough for its day, but out of date and of no great importance to anyone now? Or is there something in the Bible that people today ought to know right away? I think there is.

Let us imagine a man from some remote part of the world hearing about the Bible for the first time. He is intelligent and literate, but for some strange reason he has never before heard about this book and is curious to know what it contains that is important to him and to the rest of mankind today. He comes to me and asks what it is all about. What should I tell him? What is in the Bible that he ought to know about? What does the Bible want to say to him?

### There Is One Creator

Well, the first thing it tells him is that there is one God and that God created the heavens and the earth and everything that is in them. He created man in His own image and gave him the earth as his domain with the command to increase and multiply and fill the world with others like himself. And God made the earth so fruitful that it could easily supply food for everyone with just a little work and care on everybody's part.

### People Sinned

And then what? The Bible tells him further that man quickly rebelled against the simple commands of God and chose to run his own life without any interference from his Creator. He disobeyed God and went out on his own. The result was a bad and serious dislocation of his whole nature—body, soul and spirit—resulting in alienation from God in his heart and the final separation of body and soul in the incident we call death. He could not remain on earth and he was not fit to enter the presence of God in heaven, so God condemned him to a place previously prepared for the rebellious creatures known as the devil and his angels. That place the Bible calls hell.

### *God Rescued Us*

Was that the end of the line for the human race? No, the Bible tells the curious man that God so loved the world that He could not let men go, so He carried out a plan that He had had in His heart from the beginning of the world. He sent His Son to become one of us in the mysterious act that we call the Incarnation. The Son was and is God, but He became a man to carry out His plan of salvation. That man was Jesus Christ, whose birth we celebrate every year. We do not know the exact date, but we have fixed December 25 as the nearest we can come to it. So everywhere throughout the world Christians on that day commemorate His birth among men.

But how could He help men by merely being born a man? He could not. But there is more. After living among men for thirty-three years, He died on a Roman cross. The Romans and Jews of that time crucified Him as a common criminal, but God had another plan in mind. He let the sins of the whole world rest upon Jesus as He died, or as the ancient prophet had said, He shall "make his soul an offering for sin" (Isaiah 53:10) and His death was accepted by God for the death of every sinful man. That is what the Bible says about it. Or to quote the prophet again, "All we like sheep have gone astray; we have turned every one to his own way; and the LORD hath laid on him the iniquity of us all" (53:6).

But how can a dead man help us? If Jesus died He is no better off than the rest of men in the long parade toward the grave. Dead men cannot help dying men, and Jesus died. What does the Bible have to say about that? It says that He did not remain dead but rose from death the third day and ascended to the right hand of God to be our Lord and our Savior. This is a very important thing the Bible says here. Jesus, being very God of very God, could not long be bound by death even though the death He died was one of the most painful and degrading that mankind has ever known: the death on the cross. People ought to know this. It is a most critical truth and we cannot afford to ignore it.

The Bible tells us that God raised Jesus from the dead and made Him both Lord and Christ; and along with His exaltation He became the new Head of the human race. And how do men become members of the new human race? The Bible is very clear on this. It is by the new birth. Just as we are all born the first time into the old fallen human race, so we may be born again into a new race, like the old but different in that the new race is born of the Spirit and the old race is born of the flesh. Jesus said, "That which is born of the flesh is flesh; and that which is born of the Spirit is spirit" (John 3:6). To be born only once is to be born lost and to remain lost. To be born the second time is to be saved. This the Bible teaches and everyone ought to know about it.

***We Must Be Born Again***

But that is not all the Bible teaches about this. It tells us plainly how to be born again. Jesus came unto His own, and His own did not receive Him, it says. "But as many as received him, to them gave he power to become the sons of God, even to them that believe on his name: Which were born, not of blood, nor of the will of the flesh, nor of the will of man, but of God" (1:12-13).

The way to be born again, then, is to believe on Christ and to receive Him into our hearts as our Lord and Savior. That means that we must attach ourselves to Him in loyalty and faith. But before we can do this we must put away all our sins and confess our wrongdoings to God. The moment we do this He forgives us our sins and cleanses us from all unrighteousness. Christ then confesses our names before His Father in heaven and becomes personally responsible for us. With Him we pass out of darkness into life, and the judgment that we so richly deserved is bypassed because Christ endured it for us. The hell that was ours because of our sins was endured by Him on the cross and God will not exact justice twice for our sins. Peter put it this way: "Christ also hath once suffered for sins, the just for the unjust, that he might bring us to God" (1 Peter 3:18).

### *What the Bible Offers*

What does the Bible offer to men in Christ? The blessings are so many that it would take several books to do them justice. But here are a few: 1) God removes from us all responsibility for our past sins, these having been atoned for by the death of Christ. 2) God bestows upon us the gift of eternal life, which means the life of the eternal God in our souls. 3) We are no longer aliens but sons of God and members of the new creation. 4) He takes upon Himself the full care of our lives while we are on the earth. 5) He promises to stay with us in the hour of death and take us to be with Him in His heaven, where we will dwell forever in a state of immortality (that is, we can never die again and never be lost).

The Bible tells us also that if we will turn to Christ in full committal of faith He will give us His Spirit and we will know that we are His children by the witness of the Spirit in our hearts. So we have two ways to know that we are saved: the testimony of God's Word, which cannot be broken, and the testimony of the Spirit in our hearts. With these come a great sense of relief and a good degree of present peace and happiness which we never knew before. These things can be proved in personal experience by anyone who will turn to Christ in earnest. They are not theories, but facts demonstrable in experience.

The Bible has much more to say that is of great value to people today. But one thing I want to mention: By neglect or love of the world or addiction to sin or unbelief or unwillingness to come to Christ all these blessings may be forfeited forever. Salvation is not automatic as a result of Christ's death for all of us. Redemption was made for all of us but it is effective only toward the ones that in sincerity of heart throw themselves on the mercy of God. Those who refuse God's offer are lost eternally.

Yes, the Bible has a wonderful message for men today. For all our progress we are still people; we still need forgiveness, eternal life, a new heart and assurance of peace in the world to come. All these the Bible offers and shows how they may be secured without money and without price.

If you are interested, I would suggest that you begin today to read the Bible. Begin with the Gospel of John. Read it slowly, and as you read stop now and then and try to talk to God about what you have read. He will hear you if you are sincere. His Spirit will lead you to faith in Christ, and Christ will do the rest.

# The Bible: The Book of Life

The Bible is unique among books, which means simply that no book has been produced just like it.

The Bible is not a book of history, though it contains much history, and all it does contain is authentic.

It is not a book of science, though all its pronouncements upon the facts usually falling into the category of science are accurate and trustworthy.

It is not a book of biography, though its biographical sketches are easily the most inspiring in the world.

It is not a book of philosophy, though it is the sum of all that is deep and sound philosophy.

It is not a book of astronomy, though its references to the sun and the stars rate among the loftiest sayings ever recorded.

It is not a book of psychology, though its knowledge of the workings of the human mind astonishes the reader and lays bare his soul.

It is not strictly a book of theology, though it is the source of all the true theology this fallen world will ever know.

What, then, is the Bible? It is the Book of Life. "The words that I speak unto you," said our Lord, "they are spirit, and they are life" (John 6:63).

The Bible is a life-bringing and a life-giving book. It is not primarily concerned with any department of human thought for its own sake.

If the Bible speaks about the rainbow, it is that we may be reminded of God's covenant of mercy with mankind.

If it tells the story of Abraham, it does so that we may learn to know the place of faith in our relation to God.

If it points us to the moon and the stars, it is that we may know how frail we are.

If it talks about the birds, it is to teach us to trust our Heavenly Father without fear or doubting.

It tells us about hell not to satisfy our morbid curiosity, but that we may steer our feet far from its terrors.

It tells us about heaven that we may be prepared to enter there.

It writes the history of human disgrace that we may learn the value of divine grace.

It warns in order that it may turn our feet away from the paths that go down to the path of destruction.

It rebukes in order that we may see our own faults and be delivered from them.

Volumes could be written in praise of the Holy Bible without using one word too many. President Woodrow Wilson once said that the Bible is a book of such importance that no one unacquainted with it can be said to be an educated man, and no one who is familiar with it can be said to be uneducated. Sir Walter Scott, when he was dying, called for "the book." A servant inquired which of his thousands of volumes he meant, and the great man replied, "The Bible, of course. For a dying man there can be no other book." Even the skeptic, George Bernard Shaw, during the last years of his life, kept a Bible near him and never traveled without carrying a copy along with him.

We should all have at least two Bibles: a well-bound reference Bible for study and a large-print, plain-text Bible for devotional reading. And if we can afford it (and we can if we will cut down somewhere else), we should have a good modern translation or two. There are dozens of them. Their chief value is to stimulate interest by affording a change of style and to throw sidelights upon the text of the familiar King James Version.

Money invested in Bibles is money well spent. Time spent in reading the Bible is not likely to be time wasted. The

Bible is the supreme gift for friends and loved ones. Words spoken in favor of the Bible are good words and, if they should fall upon the right ears, might prove to be "apples of gold in pictures of silver."